BREAD THAT IS BROKEN

WILFRID STINISSEN, O.C.D.

Bread That Is Broken

~

Translated by
Sister Clare Marie, O.C.D.

IGNATIUS PRESS   SAN FRANCISCO

Original Swedish edition:
Bröd som bryts
© 1989 Karmeliterna Norraby, Tågarp

Art and cover design by Enrique J. Aguilar

Contents

Contents

Preface

It is not an easy task to write about the Eucharist. The Eucharist is such a rich and many-faceted mystery that a systematic and exhaustive treatment of it is hardly possible. Therefore, I have chosen to touch on the subject with the help of some key concepts, consider it from different perspectives, and thus continually find new aspects and dimensions.

I prefer the word "Eucharist" to the "The Lord's Supper". Eucharist is a richer word. It suggests that this sacrament is a sacrifice of thanksgiving and thus corrects the understanding that the Eucharist is only a meal. It is, besides, an ancient word that already appears in the *Teaching of the Twelve Apostles* (the *Didache*) in the second century.

All the sacraments are holy, but the Eucharist is called *Sanctissimum Sacramentum*. According to Saint Thomas Aquinas (1225–1274), all the sacraments are directed toward the "Most Holy Sacrament" as toward their goal.

The Eucharist is the Church's center, her most precious treasure. The Church is built up around the Eucharist. Yes, the Eucharist constitutes the Church. Can one complain about the Church because she keeps guard over this treasure and does not readily distribute it if she is not sure that others appreciate it as much and place as high a value on it and receive it with as great a reverence as she does?

In this small book, I will not only consider the Eucharist as the sacrament that realizes unity between Christ and the faithful; I also wish to try to show how the Eucharist is the fundamental norm for our actions. If Christ comes to us as offered, if he unites himself with us under the form of broken bread, it is for us to become like him, sacrificing, serving people.

To become one with the sacrificial Lord necessarily has consequences. The Eucharistic mystique leads to a Eucharistic ethic.

The one who wonders how he should act finds the answer in the Eucharist. He is called to become like Jesus, bread broken, "for the life of the world" (Jn 6:51).

Meal

What is most striking about the Eucharist is that one eats and drinks. The Eucharist has to do with food and drink. It does not surprise us when we know that the Eucharist points to the new creation. The new creation corresponds to the original, and in the original creation, food and drink had a central meaning.

When God created the first human couple, he said: "Behold, I have given you every plant yielding seed which is upon the face of all the earth, and every tree with seed in its fruit; you shall have them for food" (Gen 1:29). The fact that man needs to eat in order to stay alive reminds him of his fundamental dependence. His dependence on the earth is, in the final analysis, a dependence on God, because the earth is a gift that God gives to man. By eating, he affirms that he lives in communion with God.

Even the Fall of man has to do with food. It is not a matter of indifference what man eats. There is also dangerous, bad food.

"Der Mensch ist was er isst" (Man is what he eats), said Ludwig Feuerbach (1804–1872). As much of a materialist as he was, he expressed by this a deep biblical thought.

It is not unusual, then, that when Jesus comes to renew creation, he also comes with a new food. He takes Feuerbach's principle very seriously. Since we become what we eat and Jesus wants us to become completely one with him, he can do nothing else but make himself food.

"I am . . . the life", he says (Jn 14:6). He who eats of him eats life and becomes life himself. "Unless you eat the flesh of the Son of man and drink his blood, you have no life in you" (Jn 6:53).

Both the original and the new creation have, in the end, to do with food.

Bread

Jesus did not improvise the Eucharist. "I have earnestly desired to eat this Passover with you before I suffer" (Lk 22:15). He meditated for a long time on what and how he would act when his hour came. That he chose bread and wine as the Eucharistic signs was the fruit of an intensive listening to the Holy Spirit.[1]

Bread is loaded with a rich symbolism that Jesus understood. Bread is the "fruit of the earth", as the priest says when he presents the bread at Mass. The

---

[1] Cf. J.-M. Hennaux, *L'eucharistie de Jésus, fondement de l'agir chrétien* (Brussels: Institut d'études théologiques, 1972–1973), 18–21, 31–32.

bread points to the earth. It is clear from the Gospel that Jesus often pondered the grain of wheat. In the parable of the growing seed, he says: "The earth produces of itself, first the blade, then the ear, then the full grain in the ear" (Mk 4:28).

When the grain falls into the earth, it draws energies from the earth itself. It lives and develops by the help of the earth's mysterious powers. The sprout needs all the powers of heaven: rain, light, warmth, wind. The development of the seed engages all of the physical world. By the fact that so many cosmic powers are involved in the grain of wheat's growth, it could be seen as a synthesis of the whole cosmos.

The bread is also the result of "the work of human hands". There would not be bread if man did not sow, harvest, grind, knead, and bake. All of this work is or should be a concrete expression of love. Man's work is, first of all, to nourish himself. But, unlike animals, man takes his nourishment in the form of a meal. And a meal means fellowship, love. Strictly speaking, man works, not to nourish himself, but, rather, to nourish his family and loved ones. We are created to give life to others, never to ourselves.

Actually, *all* of our work should be a work of love. We work with the physical world to make life easier, not primarily for ourselves, but for others. By our work, we create possibilities for deeper fellowship. The Bible describes how the history of mankind evolves into a universal meal where all sit at the same table.

The bread, which is the fruit of man's work, symbolizes man's effort to humanize the world; an effort that is made or should be made with love.

But bread also has something to do with *Jesus himself*. He likens himself to a grain of wheat: "Unless a grain of wheat falls into the earth and dies, it remains alone; but if it dies, it bears much fruit" (Jn 12:24). The grain of wheat is entrusted to the earth but rises up later in the form of an ear. Where the original grain multiplies, so Jesus by dying and rising has brought a multitude of brothers who are like him (Rom 8:29) and who, therefore, in their turn must follow the same law of death, resurrection, and fruitfulness.

To die in order to give life: that is what we can learn from the grain of wheat.

So we see already in the Eucharist's form of bread that this sacrament has a sacrificial character.

The bread symbolizes the whole cosmos, the work of all mankind, and Jesus himself.

Luke writes that Jesus "took" bread, and when he had given thanks he broke it and gave it to them, saying, "This is my body which is given for you. Do this in remembrance of me" (22:19). The Greek word *lambano* means both to take and to receive. Jesus receives the bread from his Father. "Through your goodness," says the priest at Mass, "*we have received* the bread we offer you."

In the bread, Jesus received all of creation from his Father. When the bread is then transformed into his body, it is true, it is only that little piece of bread which is literally transformed. This is an image of the great and definitive transformation by which Jesus comes to make the whole universe into his body. He wants to "unite all things in him, things in heaven and things on earth" (Eph 1:10). Saint Paul uses the word *anakephalaioō*: to unite under one head. Jesus wants to integrate everything. He is truly "catholic": he wants to be all in all.

Every Eucharistic transformation is a step on the way toward that universal transformation where everything in the end shall be incorporated into the Body of Christ. "When all things are subjected to him, then the Son himself will also be subjected to him who put all things under him, that God may be everything to every one" (1 Cor 15:28).

By the fact that the bread refers to the whole of mankind and the whole cosmos, every Eucharist is a symbolic anticipation of that total integration. When we look at the priest taking the bread in his hands before the transformation, we ought to be aware of the fact that the Father places all of creation into the hands of the Son so that he will transform it into his body and thus divinize it.

Wine

"And likewise the chalice after supper, saying, 'This chalice which is poured out for you is the new covenant

in my blood' " (Lk 22:20). Even wine has a rich symbolic meaning. Bread is the normal, necessary food.
Wine, however, is not necessary. One could be content with water. Wine was not a daily drink in Pales-
tine but, rather, a festive drink. Wine speaks of the *joy*
of life. "Bread to strengthen man's heart" and "Wine
to gladden the heart of man" (Ps 104:15).

Wine is also a symbol of ecstasy. Wine makes man a
little crazy. "Where wine goes in, clear thinking goes
out." One who is intoxicated is "out of himself", outside of himself. He lives in another world. Therefore
wine has an eschatological meaning: the joy that the
wine brings about anticipates the joy of the world to
come. "I tell you I shall not drink again of this fruit of
the vine until that day when I drink it new with you in
my Father's kingdom" (Mt 26:29). But wine suggests
not *only* joy. In the Bible, wine is also a symbol of
God's wrath and of suffering and punishment. In the
New Testament, the chalice often means Jesus' suffering and death. "Father, if you are willing, remove this
chalice from me; nevertheless not my will, but yours,
be done" (Lk 22:42). "Shall I not drink the chalice
which the Father has given me?" (Jn 18:11).

The Eucharistic wine is a symbol of both joy and
suffering. By choosing wine as a sign of his presence
and his sacrifice, Jesus indicates that his death, despite
all the bitterness it entails, is nevertheless a source of
exuberant joy. This unity of suffering and joy is a typical Christian paradox.

Bread and wine are *vegetarian* food. When Jesus drives those who are selling oxen and sheep and doves out of the Temple (Jn 2:13–22), the meaning, among other things, is that it is now the end of animal sacrifice. In the New Testament, *Jesus himself* is the sacrifice. He is "the Lamb of God" (Jn 1:29). Vegetarian food is better suited to represent Jesus. It does not draw attention to itself. If we offered animals at Mass, we would think more of the poor animal than of Jesus.

Jesus makes himself an object, a thing. "This is my body." To make oneself an object is to die. When we die, we become a corpse, a thing. By speaking of himself as an object, Jesus speaks about his death.

Besides this, Jesus' death is a symbol indicating that the two Eucharistic signs are separated from each other. Pius XII (pope, 1939–1958) explains in his encyclical *Mediator Dei* (1947), that the two Eucharistic forms indicate the violent separation of the Blood from the Body. "The eucharistic species under which He is present symbolize the actual separation of His body and blood," he writes, "seeing that Jesus Christ is symbolically shown by separate symbols to be in a state of victimhood."[2]

At the same time that Jesus makes himself into an object signifying his death, he brings nature to life.

[2] Pope Pius XII, Encyclical *Mediator Dei* on the Sacred Liturgy (November 20, 1947, 70); See also Vatican Council II, Constitution on the Sacred Liturgy *Sacrosanctum concilium* (December 4, 1963).

The bread becomes living, it becomes man, it becomes God. "I am the living bread", says Jesus (Jn 6:51). He also shows us how we should relate to nature with respect. He teaches us the principle of a genuine ecology. Instead of polluting nature, we can do as Jesus does: let it mediate something of God's presence. The meaning of nature and creation is to point to its Creator, to speak of God, to proclaim his praise.

It is often said that God became man so that man might become God. But we can also say: God has become a part or a piece of nature so that nature might be made holy and be filled with God.

What great respect we ought to show toward nature when we see that it can become filled with God.

The Whole Mass *Is a Meal*

Just as Jesus was nourished by his Father in everything he did (Jn 4:34), so we should be nourished by Jesus. Our faith in him is itself a meal. According to many exegetes, the first part of Jesus' great discourse on the bread of life (Jn 6:34–51) is about faith in him, while the second part of the discourse focuses on the Eucharist. "I am the bread of life; he who comes to me shall not hunger, and he who believes in me shall never thirst" (6:35). Jesus considers our entire relationship to him as one of eating and drinking. Long before we have made our First Communion, we have already eaten and drunk of him by our faith.

Our whole Christian life can be considered a meal.

This is evident in the Eucharist itself, which is a summary of our life. The Eucharist begins with "The Liturgy of the Word".

Thus, we readily speak of the double table of the Eucharist: the table where we are nourished by God's Word and the table where we eat the Body of Christ.[3] "The two parts which, in a certain sense, go to make up the Mass, namely, the liturgy of the word and the eucharistic liturgy, are so closely connected with each other that they form but one single act of worship. Accordingly this sacred Synod strongly urges pastors of souls that, when instructing the faithful, they insistently teach them to take their part in the entire Mass, especially on Sundays and feasts of obligation."[4]

An Excellent School

That the Eucharist—and thus the whole of Christian life—is a meal shows us that we do not have life in ourselves. We must receive it, eat it. We become what we receive. If we refuse to receive, refuse to eat and drink him, we remain without life.

Perhaps we know theoretically that we live from Christ's life. But there is a long way to go before this intellectual truth becomes flesh and blood. The Eucharist is an excellent school where we practice this

---

[3] *General Instruction of the Roman Missal* (1969), nos. 8 and 34.

[4] *Sacrosanctum concilium*, no. 56.

truth. Every day we are reminded that we do not have the real life in ourselves, that our true life is Jesus' life in us. We need to hear and see this in external signs again and again, because we hold fast so stubbornly to our own little false idea of life.

In the Eucharist it becomes clear that you are a branch on the vine. There it becomes visible, and at the same time ever more true, that it is no longer you who live, but Christ who lives in you (Gal 2:20). Thanks to the Eucharist, it is completely clear that it is not you who take the initiative. It is he who comes to you. The only thing you have to do is eat and drink what is placed on the table. It shows that Jesus is not only Omega but also Alpha. He takes the first step. You do not need to capture him; he gives himself. He comes to you in order to be your love, your holiness. "As the living Father sent me, and I live because of the Father, so he who eats me will live because of me" (Jn 6:57).

Holiness is not an achievement but a gift. Saint Thérèse of Lisieux knew that. "I desire, in a word, to be a saint, but I feel my helplessness and I beg You, O my God! to be Yourself my *Sanctity*!"[5]

In the Eucharist we eat holiness.

---

[5] Saint Thérèse of Lisieux, *Story of a Soul: The Autobiography of St. Thérèse of Lisieux*, trans. John Clarke, O.C.D. (Washington, D.C.: ICS Publications, 1996), 276.

2

Sacrificial Meal

Before the council, the liturgy placed the emphasis on the Eucharist's *sacrificial* character. That the Eucharist was also a meal did not come across so clearly. It did not seem strange to attend Mass without receiving Communion. At some Masses, there was not even the opportunity to receive Communion. Communion was, for example, never distributed during High Mass. No one thought of fasting for the entire morning. (The Eucharistic fast began at midnight.) The eager Christians went first to an early "Communion Mass" on Sunday, then they hurried home to eat breakfast and returned to the High Mass, which was Mass without Communion.

Also the very "sign" of Communion was reduced to a minimum. The symbol had become diminished. Communicating under both species was reserved for priests. The Hosts that were distributed were very thin, and one was told never to chew them. It seems that almost everything was done so that one would get the impression that the Eucharist was not about food and drink.

After the council, the pendulum swung the other

way. Instead of considering the Eucharist as Christ's sacrificial offering, now many speak almost exclusively about a meal. It is repeated in every possible way how wonderful it is to be together, to sit at the same table. The perspective seems to have become much more horizontal. The fact that the Eucharist is also about the Father and about Christ's sacrificial offering of himself to him seems at times to have no significance.

Both Sacrifice and Meal

The Eucharist is not only a sacrifice, nor is it only a meal. It is both sacrifice and meal. It is a *sacrificial meal.* Jesus does not give us just any kind of meal. He gives us *himself* to eat and drink. He goes so completely into the bread and wine that he himself becomes food and drink.

Can one be more given, more sacrificed than to become food and drink?

In the [Extraordinary Form], which is the older form of the Mass, when the priest consecrated the bread, he said: "Hoc est enim corpus meum" (This is my body). The words "which will be given up for you" were missing. For some reason, which no historians even to this day have been able to explain, this phrase, which existed already in the time of Hippolytus (in the third century), somehow disappeared in the older form of the Mass. According to certain experts in the liturgy, this shortened version contributed to what some regard as a "static" understanding of the Eucharist. The

Real Presence was spoken of one-sidedly: the Body of Christ was truly present. But Christ's Body is more than "present". It is sacrificed, it is offered, it is given up. It is anything but static. It is blood that is flowing.

In the Ordinary Form of the Roman liturgy, the shortened formula has been replaced with the original: "This is my Body, which will be given up for you."

Ecstatic Love

In the Eucharist, Jesus shows a love that is ecstatic in the literal sense of the word. He goes out of himself, out of the limits of his body, and goes into the bread and the wine. His love is so strong that it causes him to exist outside of himself and to multiply himself. He is present in every particle of the bread he gives to the disciples.

One often represents the "miracle" of the Eucharist (transubstantiation) in an all too naïve way. One says that since God is all-powerful, he can naturally transform bread and wine into his Body and Blood. But one forgets that this divine power passes through a human consciousness.

It is not due only to the divine power of Jesus that the transformation is possible, but also because he as man loves us with a love that in its essence is "ecstatic". His love causes him to want to keep nothing for himself. The transformation is also a miracle of Jesus' human love for the Father and us. What makes the transformation possible is that Jesus dies to himself completely in order to live only for us, in a permanent ecstasy.

The Eucharist shows us that Jesus really dies of love, not only in that, driven by love, he is willing to suffer and die for us, but it is love itself that kills him. Love causes him to be thrown outside of himself, into the Father and into us. The Last Supper and the Eucharist are a perfect symbolic transcription in time and space of the Holy Trinity's ecstasy, where each Person is pure relationship and only exists in the other two.

It is in this context that the Real Presence receives its full meaning. If Jesus is not truly present under the appearances of bread and wine, then his ecstatic love is not real. Then his love is not so great, then it does not have the power really to bring him out of himself. The words that Jesus speaks: "this is my body, this is my blood" are only an expression of his desire, a sign of what he would like to do for us, but not a reality.

The dogma of the Real Presence is a dogma about Jesus' love. The fact that the Church is so emphatic about this dogma is because she knows and has experienced that Jesus' love for her is in fact so great. The Bride knows that the Bridegroom loves her *so* much. That which in the marital union is only a faint sketch, Jesus does in an absolute and definitive way in the Eucharist. It is a question of a total going out of himself.

"Do This"

"Do this in memory of me", Jesus says. According to the Council of Trent (1545–1563), Jesus institutes the priestly ministry through these words.

Jesus' words, however, are much more than an exhortation to repeat the Eucharistic ritual. When Jesus says: "Do this", he also means: Enter into the ecstatic love that I show you here, love in the same way that I love.

And again, it is Jesus' true presence (the Real Presence) that gives us a real possibility to "do this" in memory of him. He truly comes into us with all of his love, so that we *can* begin to love with his love. The Eucharist is the guarantee that we can do much more than "we are able". Instead of acting in a merely human way, we can act both humanly and divinely, because he himself comes into us. "I will not leave you desolate; I will come to you" (Jn 14:18). We may always act and love together with him.

The way we act as Christians is regulated by two fundamental words: "Without me you can do nothing", and "He who abides in me, and I in him, he it is that bears much fruit, for apart from me you can do nothing" (Jn 15:5). Every time someone comes and complains: "I have no love, I cannot love", we should be able to answer: "How can you say that, when you go regularly to Communion!"

Do we truly trust that Love himself comes into us when we receive the Eucharist?

The question is naturally *how* we receive it.

The Eucharistic Meaning of the Washing of the Feet

It has bewildered many that the Gospel of John does not give an account of the institution of the Eucharist. It is true that we find in John's Gospel the discourse of Jesus about the Bread of Life, but, in contrast to the three Synoptic Gospels, John never says that Jesus took bread and wine and said: "this is my body", "this is my blood." John, on the other hand, is the only one who mentions that Jesus stood up from the table, took off his cloak, wrapped a towel around his waist, and began to wash the feet of his disciples (13:1–17).

We find the solution to the riddle here. It is actually a Eucharistic text. Where Matthew, Mark, and Luke describe the institution of the Eucharist itself and express the words of institution, John points out the meaning of the Eucharist. The account of the washing of the feet explains for us the *reality* to which the Eucharist gives expression.

That John means something special with this account is made clear by his solemn introduction, where he emphasizes and repeats that "Jesus knew" what he was doing. "When *Jesus knew* that his hour had come to depart out of this world to the Father, having loved his own who were in the world, he loved them to the end" (13:1; emphasis added). He wants to give an extreme proof of his love. We are able to know what happens when one loves "to the end". "Jesus, knowing that the Father had given all things into his hands, and that he had come from God and was going to God" (v. 3). Jesus, who had gone out from the Father in order to gather and win back the world that had become lost to the Father, returns now to his Father with the world in his arms.

This is a decisive moment in human history. One holds one's breath: What will he do now?

To wash the feet of one's master was something that was required only of a slave who was not a Jew. A Jewish slave considered this to be inconsistent with his dignity and could not be obliged to do it. Jesus does not wash his master's feet, but the feet of his disciples. He thereby reveals God's being. God wishes to be the servant of man. He shows that service is divine. He makes clear that love is freely to become the least, to be the servant of all.

That which the Eucharistic symbols express, that he wants to become food and drink for those whom he loves, is illustrated by the washing of the disciples' feet. So that no one can misunderstand the Eucharistic symbols, Jesus makes what they refer to concrete. He is completely at the disciples' disposal. He is completely at their service.

Hans Urs von Balthasar (1905–1988) writes somewhere that the last and decisive deed of Jesus is a drama in three acts. The first act is the washing of the feet; the second, the institution of the Eucharist; and the third is Jesus' death on the Cross. These three acts are one; together they make up one drama, just as the Father, the Son, and the Spirit are one God.

The three acts of the drama have the same content, but every act expresses it in its own way. The key word that sums up the whole drama is love, or rather, extreme love. Jesus makes that extreme love clear in three different ways. Each way explains and clarifies the other two and refers to them, just as the three Persons in God point to each other and none of them can be understood without the other two. The first act shows us that love is to be the servant of all; the second, that love is to become food and drink for those one loves; and the third is that love is to give one's life.

For us, it is necessary to be a part of the whole drama in order to understand the meaning of the first act, in order to understand that love does not set any limits to its service. But on God's part, everything is said at once. Every word of his contains the stamp of his eternal nature.

The Church has always been aware of the unity between these three acts. That is why she does not hesitate to let us read the account of the washing of the feet on Holy Thursday despite the fact that on that day we celebrate the institution of the Eucharist. The washing of the feet and the Eucharist say the same thing, they express the same extreme love. And both conclude with the same exhortation: "I have given you

an example that you also should do as I have done"
and: "Do this in memory of me."

Death That Gives Life

Extreme love means death. To be so completely at the
service of others that one becomes food and drink for
them presupposes that one has died to oneself. In the
Eucharist, we are confronted with the death of Jesus
and, thereby, also with our own death, for "a disciple is
not above his teacher, nor a servant above his master"
(Mt 10:24). In Christianity, death is truly not a taboo
subject. But Christianity always sees death in connection with the resurrection. When Jesus predicts that
the Son of Man will be given over to the hands of men
and that they will kill him, he always adds: "But on
the third day he will rise again."

In the Eucharist, the Resurrection does not come
after death; rather, there is a total simultaneousness. It
is the risen Lord who is present but under the appearances of bread and wine, that is, as offered up in death.
The Book of Revelation speaks in this way about the
Lamb who appears to have been *slain* but at the same
time is standing (5:6).

For Jesus, death is not something that happens to
him but, rather, something he *does* voluntarily. "For
this reason the Father loves me, because I lay down
my life, that I may take it again. No one takes it from
me, but I lay it down of my own accord. I have power

to lay it down, and I have power to take it again; this charge I have received from my Father" (Jn 10:17–18).

Also the Second Eucharistic Prayer says that Jesus: "entered willingly into his Passion".

If we could all give our lives willingly!

For Jesus, death is an act of love, yes, the greatest love. "Greater love has no man than this, that a man lay down his life for his friends" (Jn 15:13). And love is life. As soon as one dies of his own free will and gives his life instead of having it taken from him, death is transformed into life.

To find life in the midst of suffering and death is the central message of the Gospel. This message is proclaimed unceasingly in the Eucharist. There we are able to witness continuously that suffering and death are fruitful, that the one who is willing to accept suffering and death becomes bread for others. What seemed to be meaningless, completely in vain, shows itself to be a source of the greatest fruitfulness.

Saint Luke writes that the disciples on the way to Emmaus recognized Jesus when he broke bread and gave it to them (24:30–31). The bread symbolizes Jesus. Jesus breaks and distributes himself. He is recognized in this.

One cannot distribute oneself if one has not first been broken, if one is not willing to die. Bread that is broken multiplies.

A person who understands this is no longer so resistant to all that "breaks" and afflicts him.

3

Presence

By giving himself to be eaten and drunk, Jesus satisfies his love's deepest longing: to be *in* the other.

Love is not content with only being *near*. The one who loves wants to enter into the beloved and let the beloved come in. The word "presence" is not enough to express the mutual immanence that the Eucharist brings about. We ought to create a new word and speak of "inside-ness". I pray "that they may all be one; even as you, Father, are in me, and I in you, that they also may be in us, so that the world may believe that you have sent me. . . . I in them and you in me, that they may become perfectly one, so that the world may know that you have sent me and have loved them even as you have loved me" (Jn 17:21, 23). He wills that the same intimacy that exists between the Father and himself shall exist between himself and us. The love that is eros—the love that says: "I long for you; we must be together"—reaches its highest possibilities.

Many do not understand how we as Catholic Christians can "eat" the Body of Christ and "drink" his Blood. It is like cannibalism! But everyone who loves

knows that it belongs to the essence of love to want
to be near the beloved, much nearer than our bodily
existence in time and space in fact permits. That longing which possesses all of those who love, to be completely *inside* the other, is realized in the Eucharist.

The Bridegroom Gives Himself to His Bride

When Jesus calls himself the Bridegroom (Mt 9:15),
this is not only an image. There lies a great seriousness
and deep realism in this.

In the Gospel of John, Jesus performs his first sign
at the wedding feast at Cana (2:1–11). From the very
beginning, Jesus shows himself as the Bridegroom who
celebrates a wedding with his Bride, the Church. The
fact that Mary is there and plays a much more important role than Jesus' disciples underlines, according to
Saint John's symbolism, the feminine character of the
Church. Cana is at the same time a sign of Jesus' wedding with the Church and of the Eucharist. (The best
wine is his blood poured out for us.) Cana shows that
the Eucharist has something to do with marital love.

It is typical of Saint John that he does not speak
about the Body of Christ as Saint Paul does. He uses
the word "flesh". "He who eats my flesh and drinks
my blood abides in me, and I in him" (6:56). This text,
which is so important for the Eucharist, reminds us of
the fundamental statement about marriage in the Book
of Genesis: "Therefore a man leaves his father and his
mother and clings to his wife, and they become one

flesh" (2:24). The physical union of flesh is an image, an extremely weak one, of the total union that Jesus brings about in the Eucharist with his Church and every individual believer. What the union of marriage seeks in vain to reach—namely, a total fusion and union—is realized in the Eucharist between Jesus and the Church. The Eucharist shows clearly that the Church is the Bride of Christ and that he is her Bridegroom. He gives his body to her.

This also casts light on the sacrament of matrimony. Matrimony points to the Eucharist. That is why married spouses ought to receive Communion together if possible. It is then that the sacramental meaning of their marriage becomes most clear. The union should be as faithful an image as possible of the Eucharistic union. And, seen in reverse, the Eucharistic union shows them how radical and total their union is.

Married spouses who receive Communion together demonstrate openly that they know that it is not only a natural love that unites them but that the bond between them is a third Person, Jesus Christ. He stands between the man and the wife, not in order to divide, but rather to unite them even more.

Just as a religious often reads the Rule of his Order in order to know how he should act—the Rule is usually read aloud in the refectory during meals—it is in the same way fitting for married couples to observe and be familiar with their Rule, the Eucharist. How can they image the Eucharist in their marriage if they have only an abstract knowledge of it?

The mutual immanence is symbolized even when the priest pours a little water into the wine at the beginning of the Eucharistic liturgy. The water stands for us, the wine for Jesus. Before he comes into us, we enter into him in a symbolic way. The prayer that the priest says silently while he lets the drops of water fall into the wine speaks about union: "By the mystery of this water and wine may we come to share the divinity of Christ who humbled himself to share in our humanity" (Sacramentary). The Church has always placed great emphasis on this ritual. She does not wish it to be treated lightly or neglected. It ought to awaken a certain nuptial joy in us.

There are no limits to our union with him. What God promised in Hosea: "I will espouse you in faithfulness; and you shall know the LORD" (2:20) (the biblical "to know" has marital overtones) becomes a reality in the Eucharist, much more than man could have dreamed.

Eucharistic Worship

But just as the marital union in the relationship between spouses is not permanent but a high point of love, neither is the Eucharistic union permanent.

Two people who love each other not only wish to be one, they also want to admire each other. This is not possible in the union itself. It requires a certain distance. It is the same in our relationship to the Eucharist. We do not only receive the Eucharist; we also worship it. There is a Eucharistic "inside-ness" and a Eucharistic "near-ness" (presence). We sit in front of the tabernacle or look at the Host that is exposed in the monstrance.[1]

I remember a conversation with a Benedictine Father from Chevetogne, the Byzantine Rite monastery in Belgium. He began vehemently to attack the custom of the Latin Church of exposing the Blessed Sacrament. He experienced it as repugnant and meaningless. The Eucharist is food, he said, and one should eat food and not look at it. I was influenced by his reasoning. It was shortly after the Second Vatican Council, and he formulated something that was in the air. Later I understood that he was mistaken. Food is not there only to be eaten. A meal also contains a moment of contemplation. It is truly not unimportant how the table is set, how the food is served. One begins by looking at the food, by admiring it, by giving thanks for it. If we know besides that the Eucharistic food is a Person, that Jesus Christ is truly present in it, then it is not so unusual that we would desire to gaze upon it and admire it.

Eucharistic adoration is not a medieval devotion that has seen its day. It is a treasure that we must guard carefully. Is it not significant that many new congregations and new movements give Eucharistic adoration before the exposed Sacrament an important place in their daily schedule?

[1] The custom of exposing the Blessed Sacrament came during the Middle Ages. The faithful longed to see the Lord in the Host.

The Eucharist and Ecology

Eucharistic adoration can help us to have a more proper relationship to nature. Man has become a *homo technicus* who is only out to take advantage of nature, to manipulate and impoverish it. This pragmatic attitude can even influence our way of relating to the Eucharist. It is perhaps this attitude that makes us say: "The Eucharist is food, and food is for eating." When we, on the other hand, take the time to look at the Host, to adore it, we learn a new attitude of reverence. We let reality be what it is.

Eucharistic adoration is a school in humility, silence, admiration, wonder.

After a long period of contemplating the Eucharist with reverence and worship, one cannot behave immediately after that like a despot and destroy nature. The Eucharistic bread has itself become a part of nature. To contemplate and worship it reverently necessarily influences man's attitude toward nature as a whole.

"Love as I Have Loved"

Christ is present in the Eucharist as the *living* Lord who himself wants to be our life. He not only wants to inspire our actions, he wants to act himself through us. He has said: "A new commandment I give to you, that you love one another; even as I have loved you, that you also love one another" (Jn 13:34). This "as" means more than a certain similarity or analogy. It means that we should love as radically, as boundlessly as Jesus. This is only possible when he himself loves in us.

The Christian ethic is not a list of commandments. It is a Person, Jesus himself, who through the Eucharist unites himself with us and lives in us. He constitutes the norm; he is the rule.

When it is a question of the Christian ethic, one can never be finished. The more we love, the more we realize that his love is always greater. *Deus semper maior.* It is always wrong to say "now I have done enough." His always greater love urges us always to love still more.

That is why one can never describe exactly what the Christian ethic demands. Yes, one can say: it requires love. But this very love cannot be comprehensively defined. It exceeds all words and concepts. One can only point to Jesus. But if one comes to him, one comes into a place without boundaries.

4

Agape, Self-Giving Love

What is love? Is there a more important, essential question than this? Literature, films, art, everything centers around love. There is a hunger for love in the human person, a hunger to enter into love's being, both theoretically and practically.

The Eucharist is a school in love. There we receive answers to our question. There we also have the opportunity to practice love in a practical way.

Love Is to Give Oneself

"Greater love has no man than this, that a man lay down his life for his friends" (Jn 15:13). The definition Jesus gives of love is always the maximum love. He could have said: "Love is to give", or "Love is to give something of oneself." But no, he immediately points to the greatest possible love. He is not satisfied with mediocre solutions. For him, love is to give one's life, that is, all of oneself. And he *does* it. On the Cross, he shows a total outpouring. His hands and feet, yes, and even his heart are opened so that his blood, the symbol of life, pours out unhindered and flows over the whole world. He is given, poured out, literally.

The symbols that are used in the Eucharist, active symbols—that is, symbols that realize what they signify—are in some way still more clear and radical than the original reality that they express. There is surely no more drastic way to give oneself than to let oneself be eaten and drunk by those one loves.

The Eucharist shows that love means to go out of oneself. It points to the essential reason for which we were created. "Do not get fixed on yourself", says the Eucharist; "do not pity yourself. Leave yourself, think of others, live for others." To live Eucharistically is to live for others, given, poured out, to be food and drink.

Just before we receive Communion, we pray: "Only say the word and my soul shall be healed." No sacrament is so *healing* as the Eucharist. If we are broken human beings, sick, neurotic, it is almost always because we are closed in on ourselves. It does not necessarily imply any moral guilt. But it can become guilt when we do not do anything to come out of our prison. "Lazarus, come out" (Jn 11:43), says the Eucharist. The Eucharist is a daily reminder that we are created to go out of ourselves.

By making oneself food and drink, Jesus shows that he—and in that way also the Father, for one who sees him sees the Father (Jn 14:9)—is completely given to us. Just by becoming food and drink, he can come into us and create the same outpouring love in us. He knows that we become what we eat. If we eat *agape*, self-sacrificing love, we become *agape* ourselves. What is ingenious about the Eucharist is that it at once *expresses God's* self-giving love and awakens the same outpouring love *in us*. It shows us that God is "offered", and it transforms us into "offered" people. We are allowed to be witnesses of Jesus' "ecstatic" love, and he transforms us himself into "ecstatic" people.

The Eucharist makes us an "offering . . . acceptable, sanctified by the Holy Spirit" (Rom 15:16). We are offered to God. Jesus is the sacrificial lamb, offered to the Father (during the Mass, we call him "the Lamb of God" three times), and we in our turn become small "lambs of God", offered, consecrated to God. We are seized and taken up with the great sacrificial stream that flows through the Eucharist. The Eucharistic dynamic comes out clearly in the following words of the third Eucharistic prayer. "May he make of us an eternal offering to you", the Church prays.[1]

When we speak about sacrifice, we think perhaps of small mortifications. Those who were raised in a traditional Catholic family are familiar with these small sacrifices. If one received chocolate during Lent, he saved it until Easter. It was not meaningless, even if one sometimes ate himself sick on Easter Sunday. But sacrifice is more than that. The sacrifice that God expects of us, according to the Bible, is that we do his will.

[1] Third Eucharistic Prayer, *Daily Roman Missal*, 3rd ed. (Woodridge, Ill.: Midwest Theological Forum, 2010), 797.

"Behold, I have come to do your will, O God. . . . Behold, I have come to do your will" (Heb 10:7, 9). His entire life stretches between two fundamental yes-words: Mary's "Fiat" and his own: "Not what I will, but what you will" (Mk 14:36).

To sacrifice is not primarily to do without something one actually needs. To sacrifice is to abstain from having one's own independent life. It is to wish no longer to direct your life, but to allow yourself to be led by God. One says with Jesus: "Father, into your hands I commit my spirit!" (Lk 23:46). Or with Charles de Foucauld (1858–1916):

> Father, I abandon myself into your hands; do with me what you will. Whatever you may do, I thank you. I am ready for all, I accept all. Let only your will be done in me, and in all your creatures—I wish no more than this, O Lord. Into your hands I commend my soul. I offer it to you with all the love of my heart, for I love you, Lord, and so need to give myself, to surrender myself into your hands without reserve, and with boundless confidence, for you are my Father.[2]

To sacrifice is no longer to have one's life in one's own hands but, rather, to let it lie in God's hands. One distances oneself from oneself, or, better said, from all that separates one from God.

[2] Charles de Foucauld, "Prayer of Abandonment", as translated on the EWTN website: https://www.ewtn.com/catholicism/devotions/prayer-of-abandonment-361

Sacrifice always implies death. One no longer cares about the egotistical man but rather lets him die of hunger. "If one understood the Eucharist, one would die", says the Curé of Ars (1786–1859); die, partly because the Eucharist is something so great, so overwhelming that we cannot bear it and partly because the Eucharist is Jesus' sacrifice in which we cannot participate without dying with him. When Jesus says: "Do this in memory of me", he invites us to enter into his death. To celebrate the Eucharist without being prepared to die is an inner contradiction.

"We Are God's Co-Workers" (1 Cor 3:9)

Jesus wants to lead us into his own attitude of sacrifice. It inevitably means darkness, anguish, loneliness, abandonment, and even abandonment by God. Jesus wants us to be with him. "With" is an important word. In Gethsemane, he asks the disciples to be *with* him: "Remain here, and watch *with* me", and then, "So, could you not watch *with* me one hour?" (Mt 26:38, 40; emphasis added). In the Gospel of John, it sounds even more urgent: "Father, I desire that they also, whom you have given me, may be *with* me where I am, to behold my glory" (17:24; emphasis added). We know that his glory is made visible on the Cross.

Also earlier, Jesus took the opportunity to let certain chosen people take part in his sacrifice (Jn 11:3). Jesus does not come. He waits. "Jesus loved Martha and her sister and Lazarus", writes John (11:5). And immediately after that: "So when he heard that he was ill, he stayed two days longer in the place where he was" (v. 6). These two verses belong together. Because Jesus was so close to them, he wanted them to be able to taste something of his death anguish.

Those who are closest to him are *allowed* to be with him in his suffering. Mary and John, the disciple whom Jesus loved, stand at the foot of the Cross. Mary stands there as representative for the whole Church, for each and every one of us. Everything Jesus suffers is also endured by her. She is *with* him in the absolute sense of the word.

Why is there so much suffering? Not only self-inflicted suffering—a great deal of our suffering is caused by ourselves: the one who turns away from God creates a hell for himself—but suffering that afflicts "innocent" people whose only desire is to live for God. Something of the answer perhaps lies here. Jesus wants them to be *with* him where he is.

Is that cruel? Or is it, on the contrary, an incredible gift to be *allowed* to be with him? For all eternity man will rejoice that he was allowed to be with him, that he willed to use him because his great work of salvation is also his in a *small way*. God wants to raise us up to his level. He does not treat us like infants who only receive. He wills that we should also be able to give as he does. He considers man to be his partner. He loves our sacrifices, not because he needs them, but because this brings out our greatness.

Our sacrifice proves that we are really created in

God's image, that we, like the three Divine Persons, not only receive, but also give. How could we be led into the life of the Trinity and participate in it if we could not share in their eternal giving to each other?

Let us think again of the little drop of water that is mixed with the wine at Mass. The drop of water is you and I who say: I want to be a part of this. When Peter says to the other disciples after Jesus' Resurrection: "I am going fishing", they answer: "we will go with you" (Jn 21:3). Likewise, we follow along with Jesus when he offers himself to the Father in the Eucharist.

Given to Each Other

Jesus also offers himself to man. In this aspect of his sacrificial attitude, too, he does not wish to be without us. Jesus has become broken bread for our sake. He even wishes to make us broken bread for each other and for the world. The multiplication of the loaves of which the evangelists speak must not only be a historical event. He wants to continue these miracles through us, not only by the priest who distributes the Eucharist, but by the fact that we all distribute ourselves. We may become bread ourselves as he has become bread.

Jesus was born in Bethlehem. Bethlehem means "house of bread". It already points to something of Jesus' calling: to become bread for the world. When he is born, he is laid in the manger, a place for feeding animals. Everything indicates that he is destined to become food. Bethlehem and the manger are expressive of God's patience. They point from the very beginning to what he one day in the future will literally become: food, and to that which we will also become with him: bread in the Bread. If he comes to us, it is not only to nourish us and fill us, but also to transform us into food, so that we in our turn can nourish others. We are allowed to share his responsibility and be food for the world.

To be nourished by Jesus in the Eucharist implies that we become nourishment for others ourselves. The nourishment that Jesus gives is his own love. The unbelievable thing about the Eucharist is that God's own love is given to us, not as a subject to meditate upon, not as an example to follow, but as substantial food.

If one eats and drinks this love, we become food and drink ourselves. It belongs to the essence of love to give ourselves. We begin to long to make our life a life for others. We keep less and less for ourselves, and we want to be at the service of others and make others happy. Instead of living in self-pity, we comfort others now. Instead of becoming fixated on our own sorrows, we rejoice with those who rejoice and cry with those who cry (Rom 12:15). We belong no longer to ourselves but, rather, to others. After having eaten the Body of Jesus and drunk his Blood, we ought in our turn to say, not with words but with our life: Take and eat—eat me, drink me!

If we want to know why we have a body, what the body is for, we need only look at the Eucharist.

We have received a body so that it will be given. The normal condition of the body is to be "given". Jesus comes to us in the Eucharist so that each and every one of us will be able to say: This is my body, given up for you.

It is not small things we learn in the school of the Eucharist. That is why we need many lessons; preferably daily, because every morning the Church presents us as a pure, holy, and immaculate sacrifice with Jesus. We ought to go to this school our whole life. Egocentricity and self-absorption are so tenacious that we need to be confronted again and again with the total self-giving of Jesus so as to be able gradually to overcome them.

But it is not enough to celebrate Mass like a robot or a machine. We must *know* and *live* what we do.

God's Extravagance

The Eucharist also teaches us that God is not stingy with his love.

God's way of giving is always extravagant. He does not spare anything. We see that in Cana when Jesus performs his first miracle. The bride and groom are perhaps not exactly stingy, but they have in any case planned poorly. There is not enough wine. Jesus intervenes and transforms so much water into wine—which is, moreover, of the very best quality—that it causes surprise. A wine that is so good is not served at the end of the feast!

At the miracle of the loaves, Jesus multiplies the bread, not only so that it is enough for all. Twelve baskets are filled with pieces that are left over. One need not be afraid to eat one's fill. There is always more. Love is always greater.

When Mary at Bethany pours out a large amount of precious nard on the feet of Jesus, the disciples become angry. "Why this waste?" they say (Mt 26:8). But Jesus defends Mary. He has nothing against lavishness; no, in this respect, he is never outdone.

Jesus' long farewell discourse points anew to God's extravagance. The words flow in floods over the disciples and their foolish questions. I have pointed out that the account about the institution of the Eucharist is missing in the Gospel of John, that he speaks instead in images about the Eucharist and that the washing of the feet is such an image. But the farewell discourse is also an image. Hans Urs von Balthasar describes Jesus' farewell discourse as *die Selbstverstömung des Wortes Gottes*. God's Word streams and flows over the disciples, who do not understand anything, just as the Blood flows over mankind when Jesus hangs on the Cross.

This lavishness of God teaches us that we may not be stingy with our love. We can *give* much more love than we realize, because we receive much more love than we can imagine. There is no risk that the source will *run dry*.

But despite the fact that God is so great and his love so immeasurable, he looks so *small* in that white Host.

He does not seek any attention; he does not make a show. He has no need of popularity. He is content with littleness, precisely because he is so great. His greatness is love's greatness. In the Eucharist, he is a small, hidden, almost invisible God. That is why many find it difficult to recognize him. We have become accustomed to the idea that that which is great makes a show of itself. Nevertheless, nature teaches us that the truly great things happen most often in silence. A child receives life and grows in his mother's womb in silence. The seed germinates under the earth in silence. The really great things are usually enveloped in silence.

Henri Nouwen tells how Mother Teresa (of Calcutta) once said to him that if one cannot see God in the Eucharist, one cannot see him in the poor. It is difficult to discover God in a person when he is hidden behind a perhaps unattractive exterior. The Eucharist gives us opportunity after opportunity to train ourselves to recognize God in the small and insignificant.

Nothing is so small that God cannot use it as a sign and place for his loving presence.

5

Transformation

Jesus transforms the bread into his Body and the wine into his Blood.

The Council of Trent defined that what happens at the Consecration at Mass is a real "transubstantiation". Certain Catholics believe that it would promote ecumenism if we did not insist too much on this term. To believe that Jesus is really present under the appearance of bread and the wine is, according to them, the only thing that is important. "Transubstantiation" or "consubstantiation" are theological fine points that are irrelevant.

I myself think that "transformation" is a key concept in our understanding of the Eucharist. We believe that bread and wine are *transformed* into the Body and Blood of Christ. The Protestant belief of "consubstantiation", on the other hand, means that it is true that Christ is present in the bread and the wine, but nothing has happened to the bread and the wine themselves. The bread is still only bread and the wine only wine.

Not a Destruction but an Elevation

Jesus transforms a part of nature into himself. Does that mean that he destroys nature? Does he not show a lack of respect for nature, for the bread and the wine, when he also then transforms them into his Body and his Blood?

One way of explaining the transformation could easily lead to such an understanding. One used to say that the bread ceased to be bread and the wine ceased to be wine. The bread was exchanged with Jesus' Body and the wine with his Blood. It is no longer bread—one said—but the Body of Christ; it is no longer wine, but the Blood of Christ. That which is on the paten certainly *looks* like bread, but it *is not* bread. The bread is gone, and now there is only the Body of Christ.

If one explains the transformation in this way, one suggests that the bread is definitively "dead". The bread "dies", according to this way of speaking, but it does not "resurrect". There is the death of the bread but no resurrection. But such is not our God. When he creates anew, he usually does not destroy the original creation. When he uses an earthly reality—it can be bread, wine, but also human beings (the apostles)—to make it into a sacrament, a sign of his presence, he does not do violence to the reality. He does not deny its original nature. The new creation does not contradict the first one. On the contrary. The new creation shows

and develops all the possibilities of the first creation.
God ennobles, he lifts up to a higher level. Bread does
not become inferior nourishment when it becomes the
Body of Christ. It becomes an even greater "bread";
it becomes the *true* bread. "My Father gives you the
true bread from heaven" (Jn 6:32).

The transformation is not a kind of magic, hocus
pocus by which anything whatsoever can be transformed into anything at all.[1] The bread does not lose
anything by undergoing transformation. It surpasses itself and finally becomes more nourishing than it other-
wise could have been. We ought to think in terms
of death and resurrection. The transformation of the
Consecration is not a destruction but an elevation. The
Eucharistic bread is the most genuine bread there is.

Transformation, a Fundamental Prototype

The transformation of the Eucharist is really a para-
digm, a fundamental prototype. Just as God transforms
bread and wine in the Eucharist, he also transforms human beings through justification. He does not place
a mantle over man's sins, but he transforms him so
that he becomes renewed in his very depths. From being merely human, he becomes both human and divine. The person who was first darkness now becomes
light. He becomes so filled with light that he becomes
a source of light.

[1] As is known, "hocus pocus" comes from *hoc est corpus.*

When theology speaks about sanctifying grace, it has to do precisely with this inner transformation—grace *makes* man holy. We are "partakers of the divine nature" (2 Pet 1:4).

"Be transformed", writes Saint Paul (Rom 12:2). In Greek *metamorphousthe*—one recognizes the word metamorphosis—and in Latin *transformamini*, the prefix (*meta* or *trans*) is decisive. It means that the old reality neither disappears nor ceases to be, that it is not a question of a process of substitution, as though the earthly man would be exchanged for a heavenly one. No, a sanctified person is not less of a human being but more. Then he is similar to Jesus, he who is the true human being.

Transformation is a key word. One could give many examples. We can think of the resurrection of the body. The resurrection does not mean that we receive a different body, that we lose the old and receive something completely new instead. No, it is a body "transformed" (cf. Phil 3:21), transfigured, and illumined by the Holy Spirit. It is the body that was planned by God from the beginning. That the body is not made up of the same, mortal material as our earthly body after the resurrection is of no significance. Neither is the body we have now made up of the same material as it was ten years ago, though we do not speak of a "different" body.

The relationship between the Old and the New Testament is another example. Jesus has not nullified the Old Testament. He says himself that not a single letter, not the least dot or iota, in the law shall pass away (Mt 5:18). He has not come to destroy but to fulfill (v. 17). The old is not destroyed but is taken up into a new context. When Jesus explains the Scriptures for the disciples on the way to Emmaus, he shows how the whole Old Testament speaks about him. All the events and words from the Old Testament receive a new and deeper meaning, since we Christians understand that everything points ahead to Christ. "A veil lies over their minds", writes Saint Paul about Israel. "But when a man turns to the Lord the veil is removed" (2 Cor 3:15–16). The Old Testament is explained from within. It undergoes an inner transfiguration for the one who reads it with Christian eyes.

The Eucharist Transforms Man

When the priest has presented the bread and the wine at Mass, he prays silently: "With humble spirit and contrite heart may we be accepted by you, O Lord." The bread and the wine represent the whole cosmos, but first of all ourselves, who are to be transformed. "Grant in your loving kindness", the priest prays, that "all who partake of this one Bread and one Chalice . . . may truly become a living sacrifice in Christ to the praise of your glory."[2] In the bread and the wine we present ourselves to be transformed. Just as we wish for the bread and wine to be transformed and for that

[2] The Fourth Eucharistic Prayer, *Daily Roman Missal*, 3rd ed. (Woodridge, Ill.: Midwest Theological Forum, 2010), 807.

reason they are presented to God, so also we wish to be transformed ourselves. It is the same Spirit who transforms the sacrificial gifts and all those who lift them up "with a sincere heart".[3] "Amada en el Amado transformada!" sings Saint John of the Cross (1542–1591), "the Lover with his beloved, [man] transforming the Beloved in her Lover [the Lord]."[4] This "transformation" happens principally in the Eucharist, and if we were open enough, it would also happen in reality. We can, as Saint Paul writes, be transformed into the image of the Lord and be glorified by his glory (2 Cor 3:18). Our earthly life can be transformed into a risen life. The French priest Marc Oraison, who was a surgeon before he became a priest, explained that it was the surgeon's inability to solve the problem of death that caused him to want to celebrate the Eucharist, that is, to make the resurrection present.

The transformation of bread and wine in the Eucharist teaches us that transformation is something fundamental in our lives. Everything can be transformed. It is enough to "offer" it, to lay it on the paten. The priest's gesture of sacrifice shows that the object must be lifted up and offered to God for transformation. Nothing may only lie on the earth. It must be set into a new context where it receives a new meaning. Every-

[3] Ibid., 809.

[4] Saint John of the Cross, *The Ascent of Mount Carmel*, in *The Collected Works of St. John of the Cross*, trans. Kieran Kavanaugh, O.C.D., and Otilio Rodriguez. O.C.D. (Washington, D.C.: ICS Publications, 2017), 114.

thing that we offer in the Eucharist together with the bread and the wine—our joy, our sorrow, even our sins —becomes transformed. Everything that was a minus becomes a plus. Everything becomes grace.

It ought to be easy for us as Christians to sacrifice. We are "a chosen race, a royal priesthood, a holy nation, God's own people" (1 Pet 2:9). Instead of concentrating on our poverty, our littleness, our failures, we can give all to God. He is the great transformer. But he transforms only what we give him. Bread that is not presented remains ordinary bread. Much in our life remains as it was, much stagnates, because it is not offered up.

It can happen that we struggle with certain weaknesses or sins, with character defects, psychological wounds, fear. All of this is material for transformation. Every sin can become a *felix culpa* (happy fault), every weakness a door through which God can enter into us. Every suffering can become a cross that saves us and others.

But the transformation does not happen automatically. Some small gesture is required of us, a gesture of sacrifice. The object must be lifted up and exposed to God's transforming power.

Evil Can Be Transformed into Good

This can perhaps cast light on the problem of evil. Saint Augustine (354–430) claims that evil suffers from a lack of being. He does not, of course, mean that evil does not exist—he was not so naïve—but that evil does not have any substance. God and evil are not equal. Evil is something good that has not yet found its right place or that has landed in the wrong place.

One thinks of Joan of Arc (1412–1431), who said: "God loves the Englishmen, but he does not love them in France."

There is nothing wrong with having a temper. It can even be a gift. But if the inner power is used to destroy others, if it is expressed in aggressiveness, then it becomes evil. For it to become good again, it does not need to be annihilated. It is enough to rectify the direction: instead of downward, it should be upward; instead of destructive, it should be constructive.

One understands that many of the saints had the feeling that they could have been real scoundrels. The enormous power of love they had received could have been extremely destructive if it had been directed in the wrong way. When a stream is contained within the riverbed and flows toward the sea, it is a blessing and spreads fruitfulness. But when it flows over its banks and loses the right direction, it causes damage. To spill honey on the table or on one's clothing is annoying, but honey in the mouth tastes wonderful. Egoism is a constructive force in animals, but if egoism in man is not "transformed" into love, then it has gone wrong. The important thing is that everything finds its right place.

A positive force can also be destructive when it is not used. Not to work with one's talents (cf. Mt 25:14–

30), to bury one's talent in the ground, is a source of sorrow, depression, sickness. Søren Kierkegaard (1813–1855) thinks that existential anguish is not caused by the fear of death but by the feeling that we have so much within us that we have not been able to express; life that has not been able to come forth. We feel that there is much more in us, but that it has been stifled. Anguish is a signal that says: Do not stifle the life within you, finally allow your *whole* self to "live"!

It is the task of man to let all the powers within find their place and to direct them to their proper goal. The Eucharist is the privileged opportunity for such a "transformation". Everything that has a tendency to be directed downward must be lifted up. God creates man upright, in contrast to animals, so that he can lift everything up, so that he can unite heaven and earth. We can paralyze a fellow man; we can also bless him. The same power that was directed downward is directed upward. And what a difference! "Lift up your hearts!" says the priest. Do we do that? Everything that weighs us down, all that blocks our development, we ought to lift up in a gesture of sacrifice. In that way, we show that we want to restore the right direction. We show our good will. We make a small attempt. The actual transformation is brought about by God. But once again, nothing is transformed that is not first offered up.

A great deal would happen in our lives if every time we celebrated the Eucharist, we would place on the paten something of our own, something that we know is directed wrongly and that therefore blocks us. It would help us to be more engaged in the Eucharist, to break the routine. It would also allow us to live consciously, to learn to know ourselves better, to live more in the truth. It would, above all, contribute to a progressive "transformation". As long as it is only the bread that is transformed, the Eucharist does not have its full effect. Bread does not merely represent itself. That is why the Church speaks of "the work of human hands" in the offertory prayer. Man is involved. Objectively. He ought to be so subjectively also, consciously.

We imagine all too often that we must offer beautiful things to God. But the beautiful does not need to be offered to God. It is already in God's sphere. It is the evil, that which has not yet found its right place that must be lifted up and placed there where it belongs, in God's radiance.

The Cosmic Dimension

Not only man and what belongs to him can and ought to be transformed. All of creation is affected by transubstantiation. The Eucharistic transformation has a cosmic dimension. Bread and wine are a part of nature. The Consecration means a transformation of nature. It points to what nature, yes, even the whole cosmos is destined to become. We read in the creation narrative that God saw that what he had created was "very good" (Gen 1:31). It was good because it was transparent. Everything created was a sign of his presence and love. When the Bible says that God blessed creation, it means that he lets creation mediate something of his love and glory. He gives creation a language that allows it to speak of him. "The heavens are telling the glory of God; and the firmament proclaims his handiwork. Day to day pours forth speech, and night to night declares knowledge. There is no speech, nor are there words; their voice is not heard; yet their voice goes out through all the earth, and their words to the end of the world. In them he has set a tent for the sun, which comes forth like a bridegroom leaving his chamber, and like a strong man runs its course with joy" (Ps 19:1–5).

In the garden of Eden, man understood the language of creation. By God's commission, Adam gives names to all living creatures (Gen 2:20). To give a name to something means, in biblical language, to express the essence of that thing. Adam understands what creation is saying; he sees that everything is a gift from God and proclaims his love. What makes up the essence of creation is that it is in one way or another a revelation of God. Adam is the priest of all of creation. He listens to the language of creation and transposes it into human words. It is his role to sing a song of praise and thanksgiving that sums up and interprets everything that creation wants to tell about God.

When man sins, he loses that ability to understand creation's language. He no longer sees that creation is a sacrament of God's presence and that that is the world's only meaning. The world becomes mute, or, better said, man becomes deaf. The world is now for him no more than dead matter.

But then Jesus comes. God becomes man. He becomes "flesh", matter. God shows concretely and tangibly that matter is not as opaque and rough as we thought. The material world is great, for God has become a part of the world. That God became "flesh" indicates that matter is open to receiving the divine, that it can be penetrated by divinity. The transfiguration of Christ is a striking example of this possibility for matter to become completely translucent. Jesus is not bathed in glory, but it is his very own body that begins to shine. "His garments became glistening, intensely white, as no fuller on earth could bleach them", writes Saint Mark (9:3). Matter itself becomes flooded and filled with the divine presence.

And then Jesus institutes the Eucharist. He takes bread—symbolically, he takes the whole world—in his hands and says: "This is my body." What Adam neglected, and because of sin also became incapable of doing, namely, to recognize God's presence in creation, Jesus does. Creation is my body, he says. He restores the original order. But as always, the new order becomes more beautiful, richer, "more wonderful" than the original.[5] The world not only speaks once more about God and his presence, but certain parts of the

[5] In the preconciliar Mass, the Church prayed: "O God, who wonderfully created human nature and still more wonderfully renewed it [*mirabilius reformasti*]".

world become themselves God. And these parts show that the world in its entirety is destined to enter into Christ's body.

In the Eucharist, the whole world is given back to man, but now it sings yet more beautifully than it did in the garden of Eden.

The Incarnation and the Eucharist, which is the extension of the Incarnation, give us a new perspective on the world, a perspective of which even Adam in his innocence could not have dreamed. The world sings once again about God, yes, but it also bears within itself a secret longing to do and become more. It wants to become the body of Christ! We understand Saint Paul when he writes that "the whole creation has been groaning with labor pains together until now" (Rom 8:22). And the world's longing is answered. For "from the rising of the sun to its setting", the priest of the Church takes bread and wine and says: "This is my Body, this is my Blood."

6

Thanksgiving

"And he took bread, and when he had given thanks he broke it and gave it to them, saying, 'This is my body which is given for you. Do this in remembrance of me'" (Lk 22:19). For a believing Jew, it is normal and obvious to thank God before or during a meal. He knows that the bread is a gift from God and therefore thanks the Creator of the world who created him and continues to create through this bread.

Thanksgiving during the Last Supper however, is much more than this.

The Great Thanksgiving

The Last Supper is the *great* thanksgiving. In a sublime prayer of thanksgiving, which is usually called the high priestly prayer (Jn 17), Jesus thanks the Father not only for the bread and the wine, but for his whole life and for everything.

We may not forget what is said about the symbolism of the bread. Bread symbolizes the whole cosmos, man's work, the entire history of mankind. It is *this whole reality* that Jesus receives from his Father when he takes the bread that is on the table into his hands, and it is for all of this reality, for this total gift, that he thanks his Father. The Father gives the whole of creation to Jesus so that he can make it his body, his mystical body.

When man receives bread from God, he receives his life, his body, because the body cannot live without this food. But here at the Last Supper, Jesus receives from the Father not only his physical body, but his total, universal body, a body that is as great as creation. "All that is yours is mine", says Jesus to his Father (see Jn 17:10). Nothing is excluded. Creation in its totality is given to Jesus by the Father. It is for this that Jesus gives thanks at the Last Supper.

We can perhaps understand better the inner connection between the mystery of the Incarnation and what Saint Paul writes about the mystical body of Christ. If the Word became flesh in a single, physical body, it is in the final analysis in order to make all of mankind and the whole universe into his mystical body.

The goal of the Incarnation is for all of reality, everything created, to become the body of Christ.[1]

Active and Engaged Thanksgiving

The Father gives everything to Jesus, and Jesus gives thanks for everything. His gratitude is as great as the Father's gift. But he does not give thanks only with

---

[1] Cf. J.-M. Hennaux, *L'eucharistie de Jésus, fondement de l'agir chrétien* (Brussels: Institut d'études théologiques, 1972–1973), 22–23.

words. His thanksgiving is an act that engages him completely. Since the Father gave all of creation to Jesus so that he could make it into his body, Jesus cannot receive this gift in a purely passive way. The Father's gift is not like an ordinary present that one holds in one's hands and admires but is in any case foreign, something that is and remains outside the being of the receiver. Jesus' thanksgiving consists of him *actively making* creation into his body; he goes into it so that it becomes his own. "Make this your body", says the Father. "This is my body", Jesus answers, and thereby makes the bread into his body. So far it is only the bread that is literally transformed into Jesus' body. But since the bread symbolizes the universe, the whole universe is symbolically taken up and integrated into Jesus' body. Every Eucharist shows us, in a symbolic sign, that creation in its entirety is destined to become Jesus' body.

That Jesus *makes* the bread his body *is* his thanksgiving. It is the way that he shows that he really receives the Father's gift according to the Father's intentions. At the same time, he lets the gift flow back to the Father. The one who gives thanks says: it comes from you, it is yours. By making the bread, and symbolically all of creation, into his body, Jesus gives everything back to the Father. As soon as it is his body, it is also the Father's. For "all mine are yours" (Jn 17:10). By making the world into his body, he restores it and brings it back to the Father.

The Eucharist Is a Prayer of Thanksgiving

The Eucharist is the great thanksgiving. The Second Vatican Council emphasized this truth. It also comes out clearly when we speak of the Eucharistic Prayer, that is, the prayer of thanksgiving (*eucharistein* means to thank), and this prayer is the central part of the Mass.

The Eucharistic Prayer begins with a triple dialogue between the priest and the congregation: "Let us give thanks to the Lord our God", and the congregation answers: "It is right and just." And then comes the priest's enthusiastic response: "It is truly right to give you thanks, truly just to give you glory, Father most holy." This first part of the Eucharistic Prayer, which is called the preface, sets the tone. Everyone who has ears to hear understands that what now begins is a prayer of thanksgiving.

Unfortunately, the word *praefatio* has often been translated wrongly as "introduction" or "foreword". A foreword does not belong to the book. The book begins with chapter one. The Jesuit Father Joseph Jungmann (1889–1975), one of the Catholic Church's foremost experts on the liturgy, has shown that the word *praefatio* means here to stand and speak on someone's behalf. Just as the father of the family stood and spoke to God about all his great deeds during the Jewish Passover meal, the priest stands before (*prae*) God and speaks solemnly to him (*fari* often has an overtone of solemnity). The preface is a part of the Eucharistic Prayer, and an important part, because it so clearly expresses the meaning of the whole action.

Since bread and wine symbolize creation in its entirety, we give thanks for everything. Our thanksgiving receives a universal dimension that becomes especially clear in the Fourth Eucharistic Prayer. We thank God that he has created man in his image, that he entrusted the world to his care, that he came to the help of all peoples, that he offered his covenant and taught man to hope for salvation through the prophets, that he sent his Son to save us, that his Son gave himself up to death and so brought the power of death to nothing and renewed life, that the Son sent the Holy Spirit who will "graciously sanctify these offerings, that they may become the Body and Blood of our Lord Jesus Christ."

Thanksgiving presupposes remembrance. We remember all of God's good deeds that reach their high point in Jesus' suffering, death, and Resurrection. Church Latin has a special word to indicate this remembrance, namely, *memoriale*. It differs from an ordinary remembrance by the fact that the past event does not only belong to the past but is actualized and present in the now. God carries out his saving work right in our midst, here and now.

Sacrifice of Thanksgiving

In the Eucharist, we do not give thanks only with words. The Eucharist is a *sacrifice* of thanksgiving. We give, we offer something to God to thank him for what he has given us. And what we give him is the finest, most precious there is: the Body and Blood of Christ. God has given us his Son, and we give back to him his Son. We always have the Body and Blood of Jesus at our disposal, and therefore we can thank the Father in an adequate way.

We can give him something truly worthy of him. We do not need to be ashamed when we thank God in the Eucharist. We truly have something to offer.

Saint Mary Magdalen dei Pazzi (1566–1607), a Carmelite nun in Florence, has left us an exquisite prayer to Mary. If we change "Mary" to "Father", it expresses exactly what we mean here: "O Father, what should I be able to give to you that you are willing to receive? If I gave you my will, I fear you would not care about it, because it is not in accord with yours. If it were my spirit, it is not enlightened. If it were my memory, it forgets your good deeds. If it were my love, it is not pure. Therefore I will give you the heart of your only Son, and may the one who can give you a greater gift do so!"

The Eucharist: Both God's Gift and Ours

Is the Eucharist God's gift to us or our sacrifice to God? It is, as so often in Christianity, a both/and.

> God's gift does not exclude but, on the contrary, liberates our gifts to God [writes Hans C. Cavallin]. God's gift is so great, God's grace so fantastic, God's deed so totally transforming, that it makes man free to give a response, which is both completely a work of grace and truly his own. Saint Augustine said that when God crowns the merits of the saints, it is his own gifts that he crowns.[2] In a fundamental Bible verse, it says: "But who am I, and what is my people, that we should be able thus to offer willingly? For all things come from you, and of your own have we given you" (1 Chron 29:14). And in the First Eucharistic Prayer: "We, your servants and your holy people, offer to your glorious majesty from the gifts that you have given us. . . ." The Eucharist is both God's gift and our gift to God. . . . For Christ is both God's gift to us and man's gift to God.[3]

We are like children who receive money from our mother to buy her a birthday present when she has a birthday. When the children come with their gift, the mother does not say: "You ought to be ashamed of

---

[2] The renewed liturgy quotes this text in the first preface for the saints.

[3] *Svensk Pastoral Tidskrift*, no. 45 (1976): 826–27.

yourselves to come with a gift that I myself have paid for!" No, she acts as though it were from them. She appears and also is happy for the children's gift. That is what God does with us. Everything we give him we have received from him. Nevertheless, he acts as though everything came from us.

Our thanksgiving consists in that we give everything back to God. "God gives us many things only so that we will sacrifice them to him. He himself assumed a body only in order to sacrifice it on the Cross and nourish us with it", writes Hans Urs von Balthasar.[4] It is not because God is greedy and therefore wants everything back, but rather so that we should have the *joy of giving*.

A School of Thanksgiving

In the Eucharist, we participate in the heavenly thanksgiving where Jesus with his rich and beautiful voice sings *cantus firmus* and all the angels and saints sing and play along in an endless number of parts and with countless instruments. We are united with our brothers and sisters in heaven and try to sing as well as we can in order not to disturb the heavenly harmony.

It is truly great to know that we do not do this alone. We are part of and are carried by the heavenly liturgy. Every preface finishes with expressing our conviction

[4] Hans Urs von Balthasar, *The Grain of Wheat: Aphorisms*, trans. Erasmo Leiva-Merikakis (San Francisco: Ignatius Press, 1995), 46.

that it is together with the angels and saints that we sing: Holy, holy, holy.

But we do more than that. We also give a voice to creation. "And so, in your presence are countless hosts of Angels, who serve you day and night and, gazing upon the glory of your face, glorify you without ceasing. *With them we, too, confess your name in exultation, giving voice to every creature under heaven,* as we acclaim, Holy. . . ."[5] We stand between heaven and earth, and our task is to unite them.

In our day, it has become difficult to give thanks. We have more interest in the weeds than in the wheat. We have lost the child's ability to wonder and be amazed. We would rather protest, demonstrate, and revolt than give thanks.

The Eucharist is a school of thanksgiving. There we learn again to give thanks, not only for the beautiful and delightful, but also for the difficult, for suffering and death. United with Jesus, we give thanks for his death, which has become our salvation, and thereby we give thanks also for our own death. To celebrate the Eucharist is like saying with Thomas: "Let us also go, that we may die with him" (Jn 11:16).

The Eucharist can teach us to give thanks for *everything*. "Give thanks in all circumstances; for this is the will of God in Christ Jesus" (1 Thess 5:18). There is a shining example of this: Mary. Her "magnificat" is a

---

[5] Fourth Eucharistic Prayer (emphasis added).

Eucharistic hymn, a song of thanksgiving. Who does not think of the Eucharist when he hears Mary sing that God fills the hungry with good things (Lk 1:53)? In Mary's life, everything becomes a source and cause of thanksgiving.

7

Unity

God has revealed the mystery of the Trinity, among other reasons, to help us understand that life is only real life if it is shared with others. Authentic life is always shared life. "Sein ist mit-sein" (Martin Heidegger, 1889–1976). "Shared joy is double joy", according to a familiar saying. Perhaps it is more correct to say: *Only* shared joy is real joy.

Created for Communion

As a Christian, one ought to ask oneself often: *Am* I communion?

God is *koinonia*, communion. He is family, he is friendship. He is not a mathematical unity. If he were that, his being would consist of a narcissistic self-reflection. God's unity is a unity of love. It is harmony, concert, music. He has created us in order to allow us to participate in that harmony, so that we will be one with him and, in that way, with one another.

Sin has divided us. We are not a community any longer, but individuals who think of themselves, rather than of the community. Through sin, loneliness has come into our lives. Sin always causes loneliness.

But Jesus has come to restore unity. His task is to gather us again. It is typical that the word "gather" appears so often in the Gospels and even already in the Old Testament. "Jesus should die for the nation, and not for the nation only, but to gather into one the children of God who are scattered abroad", writes Saint John (11:52). "He who is not with me", says Jesus, "is against me, and he who does not gather with me scatters" (Mt 12:30). To be with him is always to gather. "Jerusalem, Jerusalem, killing the prophets and stoning those who are sent to you! How often would I have gathered your children together as a hen gathers her brood under her wings, and you would not!" (Mt 23:37). Every Christian has the mission to gather.

The Sacrament of Unity

There is one sacrament that more than all the others expresses and strengthens this unity, namely, the Eucharist. "Eat this sacred food, so that your bond of unity with Christ may never be broken", writes Saint Thomas Aquinas in the Divine Office for the Solemnity of Corpus Christi.[1]

---

[1] "Ne dissolvamini, manducate vinculum vestrum" ("Eat this sacred food, so that your bond of unity with Christ may never be broken"), from *The Liturgy of the Hours*, vol. 3 (New York: Catholic Book Publishing, 1975), 611.

Jesus has chosen *bread* as a sign for his body. This already indicates that the Eucharist is the sacrament of unity. Many Church Fathers have pointed out that bread comes into being by the fact that man combines many grains of wheat, which are then ground, kneaded, and baked and so become *one* substance. In the *Didache* (the *Teaching of the Twelve Apostles*), we read: "As this broken bread was scattered over the hills, and was gathered together and became one, so let Thy Church be gathered together . . . from the ends of the earth into Thy kingdom."[2]

So bread reflects the mutual unity of all mankind, and this exists already before the transformation. There is in the bread itself a hint of what the Constitution on the Sacred Liturgy says about the Eucharist, that it is "a sign of unity, a bond of charity".[3]

In the Catholic Church, we do not speak about sharing in the Lord's Supper but about "going to Communion", and it is preferable that we continue to speak in this way. "To go to Communion" is a beautiful and significant expression. It means not only—as many believe—that we are united with Jesus, but that we enter into community. *Communio* is the Latin word for *koinonia*. Similar to the three Persons of the Trinity,

---

[2] *The Teaching of the Twelve Apostles*, 9.4–5, in *Ante-Nicene Fathers*, ed. Alexander Roberts and James Donaldson, vol. 7 (1886; Peabody, Mass.: Hendrickson, 1995), 380.

[3] Vatican Council II, Constitution on the Sacred Liturgy *Sacrosanctum concilium*, (December 4, 1963), no. 47. The Constitution quotes Saint Augustine.

all Christians together make up a *koinonia*. It is this *koinonia* that we enter into by "receiving" Communion. It is above all in and through the Eucharist that the Church becomes herself; namely, community, an icon of the community of the Trinity.

Community is realized most clearly in the Eucharist. It is there that it is closest and most intimate. "Really partaking of the body of the Lord in the breaking of the Eucharistic bread, we are taken up into communion with Him and with one another", says the Constitution on the Church, referring to the famous passage of Saint Paul: "Because there is one bread, we who are many are one body, for we all partake of the one bread" (1 Cor 10:17).[4]

By eating one and the same bread, we become companions. "Companion" comes from *cum* and *panis*: to eat bread together. Instead of "companion", we now prefer to say friend. To eat the same bread makes us friends, companions, followers. We are engaged in the same adventure. The sign that Saint Peter gives to prove that he belongs to those "witnesses" is precisely the fact that he "ate and drank with him after he rose from the dead" (Acts 10:41).

But since the bread in the Eucharist is the Body of Christ, our mutual unity becomes immensely deeper than when we eat ordinary bread together. We cannot be incorporated into the Body of Christ without at the same time being incorporated into each other.

[4] Vatican Council II, Dogmatic Constitution on the Church *Lumen gentium* (November 31, 1964), no. 7.

The one who becomes one with the head of the body also becomes one with the body's members.

In the Eucharist, we become liberated from our deepest loneliness. When I receive the Eucharist, Jesus' suffering and death become a suffering and death for me. God's love becomes a love for me. I become a part of the Body of Christ. I can say "you are mine" to him. And by the fact that everyone who receives the Eucharist can say the same thing, we all become members. We enter into a new world where we share everything with each other.

There can never be a reason for rivalry or envy any longer, since we have become communicating vessels in the Body of Christ. If I am envious of another because he or she has received more than I have, it proves that I have not understood anything of the new physics that reigns in the Eucharistic world. The name of this new physics is *communio*: no one receives anything only for himself; everyone has everything in common. What you have is also mine; what I have is also yours. Envy is replaced by joy and gratitude.

"You Shall Love One Another"

Precisely because the Eucharist is the sacrament of unity and love, Jesus at the same time gives his new commandment about love when he institutes this sacrament (Jn 13:34).

What can make receiving Communion a sacrilege is not that one somehow harms the utterly holy God by receiving him into a stained soul. The glorified Christ cannot be sullied. That a particular Communion becomes a sacrilege is due to the fact that it is a grave lie to approach the sacrament of unity with God and each other while one clings to sin. Sin is in its essence division, a breaking of the bond of love that binds us to God and to each other. Thus we understand that we cannot receive Communion if we are not willing to be reconciled with God and each other.

The Eucharist does not create automatic unity. In the Gospel, the washing of the feet precedes the institution of the Eucharist. Only when we are prepared to wash one another's feet, that is, to serve one another, can the Eucharist fulfill its unifying role. The Eucharist is not some kind of magic that can conjure up unity. Some seem to believe that when they expect too much from intercommunion.

We ought to be extremely sensitive to everything that breaks or injures unity. There is something dishonest in eating the Body of Christ and drinking his Blood together with people with whom one is not reconciled from one's very depths.

Our first task as Christians is to establish peace, to forgive, to live in love between us.

The Eucharist leaves us no choice (cf. 2 Cor 5:14).

8

Eschatology

It is repeated again and again in the New Testament that the end times have already come about through Jesus Christ. The theologians call this "eschatology" (*eschaton*—the end, the last). The meaning is, of course, not that history is finished, but that history's decisive event has already occurred in and with Christ.

This decisive event is present among us in the Eucharist. Jesus himself describes the Eucharist as an eschatological reality. He calls it the "the food which endures to eternal life, which the Son of man will give to you" (Jn 6:27). He who eats the true bread from heaven shall never hunger or thirst again (6:32, 35). "He who eats my flesh and drinks my blood *has* eternal life, and I will raise him up at the last day" (6:54; emphasis added). The Eucharist belongs to eternity, to the final, definitive life.

The Future Becomes the Present

In the Eucharist, the goal of the world and mankind is present. There everything has already reached its goal; there we are directly confronted with history's end.

The parousia (Jesus' return) has begun; it is already real. The Eucharist is "sacramental parousia", that is to say, in the Eucharist the parousia is present in a sacramental, "effective" sign.

The *eschaton* of creation (the goal, end, and definitive state) is nothing other than Jesus Christ, glorified by his death, who gathers and integrates everything in himself. As such, we encounter him in the Eucharist. "*Today* you will be with me in Paradise", says Jesus (Lk 23:43; emphasis added). The Gospel's message to the Jews and us is: the paradise that we await has already come.

John the Baptist says about Jesus: "Behold, the Lamb of God" (Jn 1:29). This Lamb of God, he who redeems man from his sins, *behold*, he is here. In and with Christ, the end has come, for, in and with him, God's plan has become reality. Since he has come, creation has succeeded and reached its goal.

Where the Eucharist is, there Jesus is truly present; there the Church and finally all of creation are already one body; there we already have a share in eternal life. To receive the Eucharist is to enter into the joy of the Lord (Mt 25:21), to go up to heaven. Adam is taken again into paradise. He brings back all of creation to God and gives thanks, gives thanks . . .

Just as on Mount Tabor Jesus anticipates and shows the glory he will receive through his death and Resurrection, so the Eucharist anticipates the transformation and the transfiguration of the world.

Both "Completed" and "on the Way"

"It is finished", says Jesus (Jn 19:30). Does this mean that history is concluded, that we no longer have anything to do, since everything has been done by Jesus, that there is no place for hope any longer, since all is absolutely completed?

Here again, we ought to be careful not to make a false formulation of the question. Even here it is, as so often in Christianity, both/and. It is both "finished" and "on the way to being fulfilled".

> It is sometimes said [writes Hans C. Cavallin] that the consequence of the Catholic perspective that all the faithful present themselves as an atoning sacrifice to the Father for the world through Christ is that the sixth word of Jesus on the Cross ought to have been: "It is not finished." The answer is that the total Christ is Christ *and* the Church: the Head *and* the Body. It does not mean a late medieval distortion that the Church's gifts or work would be able to add anything to the one sacrifice of Christ once and for all; rather, it means that in Christ's sacrifice on Golgotha, Christ's Body the Church is offered together to the Father. The Eucharist means the realization of this sacrifice once and for all, that the Church goes anew outside of time into eternity and thereby reaches the central point in history, which is Golgotha. But every suffering, every thought, word, and deed of a member of Christ's Body is already incorporated into Christ's

sacrifice and can *consciously* be given as a sacrifice in, with, and through that sacrifice. That is why Saint Paul writes: "Now I rejoice in my sufferings for your sake, and in my flesh I complete what is lacking in Christ's afflictions for the sake of his body, that is, the Church" [Col 1:24].[1]

The Typical Christian Behavior

Just as eschatological reality gives us a clear criterion that allows us to judge and distinguish what authentic Christian behavior is, so also does the Eucharist.

The traditional moral teaching taught us that it is the action's relationship to man's final goal (*finis ultimus*) that decides its moral quality. An action is good when it is in harmony with or leads to the final goal. It is evil when it prevents the development toward that goal. And the goal is the highest good, God.

This was rather abstract and was valid just as much for non-Christians as for Christians. It was, moreover, inherited from Aristotle (384–322 B.C.).

In the Eucharist, on the other hand, the definitive goal of mankind and history becomes concrete and present. The Eucharist is itself the eschatological reality. It is now possible to test every action, every idea, philosophy, every institution, every political system, against the Eucharist. We now have an extremely concrete reference point.

What is our final goal according to the Eucharist?

[1] *Svensk Pastoral Tidskrift*, no. 45 (1976): 827–28.

1. *God.* But God is no longer abstract now. We are called, like Jesus, to be completely offered to the Father. Jesus was obedient unto death and, in that way, showed that the Father's will is so great, so holy, that one obviously sacrifices everything for it, even one's life. Nothing may be withheld from the Father.

And just as Jesus in the Eucharist does not only offer himself, but, as cosmic high priest, he gathers together everything that existed before him and that comes after him in order to present it to the Father as a thanksgiving offering, so we can be creation's priests, his concelebrants, and in communion with him offer everything created to the Father. Everything created can become holy, consecrated to God, and in that way receive back its right relationship to God.

Nothing may remain outside: "I . . . will draw *all men* [according to another version, *everything*] to myself" (Jn 12:32). Everything can be placed in that current. An action that keeps itself outside that current is not Eucharistic and therefore not Christian. For a Christian, there can be no indifferent action (*actus indifferens*). This old matter of dispute within moral theology is resolved by the Eucharist. *Everything* shall be directed to God.

2. *Universal unity.* In the Eucharist, universal unity is already a fact. Since the bread symbolizes all of mankind, Jesus lets all mankind become a part of his Body when he transforms the bread into his Body. I pray "that they may all be one", he says to the Father

(Jn 17:21). In and through the Eucharist, that prayer is fulfilled.

But even here, what he has done objectively and subjectively must be accepted by us. To receive the Eucharist is to enter into the universal community. It would be a lie if our actions did not witness to unity and community. Every action that divides or wounds is un-eucharistic. The Eucharist drives us to work for unity, in our families, our community, our diocese, in relationships between the churches, in politics. The Eucharist teaches us to conquer the "master-slave" dialectic that usually controls politics. The demand for *power* must be replaced with the willingness to *serve*. "You call me Teacher and Lord; and you are right, for so I am" (Jn 13:13–14). Power becomes service; the master becomes servant. We find the same thing in the Synoptic Gospels. In Luke, Jesus describes in detail what "Eucharistic" politics should look like: "The kings of the Gentiles exercise lordship over them; and those in authority over them are called benefactors. But not so with you; rather let the greatest among you become as the youngest, and the leader as one who serves. For which is the greater, one who sits at table, or one who serves? Is it not the one who sits at table? But I am among you as one who serves" (22:25–27).

Jesus turns everything upside down. The relationship between people and nations should be marked by a desire to serve.

Our desire for power becomes radically undermined

by the Eucharist! The one who lives and thinks Eucharistically always finds himself in the last place.

3. *Communion with the whole universe.* Not only mankind, but the entire cosmos is destined to become a part of Jesus' Body. This cosmic communion is anticipated in the Eucharist. We see concretely how God takes a part of nature and transforms it into his body. We begin to understand how great nature is since it *can* become Jesus' Body.

We learn to treat nature with respect, to use it so that it becomes a sign of God's presence. We begin to realize that it is an offense to do violence to nature, that there must be limits to man's manipulation of nature. He who does not respect creation is lacking in reverence for the Creator.

The Eucharist also teaches us that we all share in this world's concrete reality. In principle, all are invited to the Eucharist. The transformed bread is not only for the rich. The unjust distribution of the world's goods, which is the great scandal of our time, is deeply uneucharistic. The Eucharist teaches us that everyone has the same right to share in and receive food and drink. The Eucharist is a constant stimulus to work for a more just distribution of the world's resources.

Unity and Reconciliation

The Eucharist creates unity *within ourselves* by the fact that it allows us to offer *everything* to the Father. There is no risk of inner division or dualism when all flows in the same direction. The Eucharist creates unity *between God and us*. God becomes our food. A greater unity is not imaginable. The Eucharist creates unity *between people* by the fact that we are all nourished by the same food. The Eucharist creates unity *between us and the world*. What we eat is transformed bread; what we drink is transformed wine. We nourish ourselves with a world that is made holy.

The Eucharist is *cosmic reconciliation*. What Saint Paul writes about Christ, that he is our peace, that he has broken down the dividing wall of hostility (Eph 2:14), receives a completely special significance when we think of the Eucharistic Christ. "In him all things hold together" (Col 1:17). Saint Paul speaks of the plan God had from the beginning and that would be carried out when the time had come (the time is the Eucharist's time) to unite all things in Christ, things in heaven and things on earth (Eph 1:9–10). Or, with the words from the Letter to the Colossians: "For in him all the fulness of God was pleased to dwell, and through him to reconcile to himself all things, whether on earth or in heaven, making peace by the blood of his cross" (1:19–20).

We have the fruit of this plan in our midst: in the Eucharist.

9

The Eucharist and the Church

"I'm deeply convinced", writes Henri Nouwen, "that the greatest spiritual danger for our times is the separation of Jesus from the church. The church is the body of the Lord. Without Jesus there can be no church; and without the church we cannot stay united with Jesus. I've yet to meet anyone who has come closer to Jesus by forsaking the church."[1]

Mary's Yes and the Church's Yes

Jesus and the Church are one. The Eucharist does not come into being without the Church. Jesus cannot "transubstantiate" the bread without the Church's Yes. He cannot enter into mankind and make her his body, his Bride, if the Bride does not say Yes.

Just as the Incarnation was impossible without Mary's Yes at the Annunciation, so also transubstantiation is impossible without the Church's Yes. And the Church's Yes is an extension of Mary's Yes. Jesus can only show

[1] Henri J. M. Nouwen, *Letters to Marc about Jesus: Living a Spiritual Life in a Material World*, trans. Hubert Hoskins (New York: HarperOne, 2009), 83.

his "extreme" love when it is received and accepted by an "extreme" Yes, a Yes without a shadow of a No, an "immaculate" Yes.

That is why Fra Angelico (ca. 1387–1455) allows Mary to be present at the Last Supper. She cannot be completely absent. She is found somewhere in a corner. Her Yes makes it possible for Jesus to give himself to his Church.

It is in Mary's absolute Yes that the disciples participate when they receive their first Communion, each one in his own way, according to the measure of his faith and his love. By receiving Jesus' Eucharistic Body, they show that they want to live in intimate union with him. "You are those who have continued with me in my trials", Jesus says to them (Lk 22:28). They will abandon him, it is true—except for John, who more than all the rest stands near Mary—but their cowardice is passing. If Jesus foretells that Peter will deny him, he also predicts that after this Peter will be faithful to him again: "But I have prayed for you that your faith may not fail; and when you have turned again, strengthen your brethren" (Lk 22:32).

Jesus desires to make the disciples into his Body *before* he enters into his suffering and death. The disciples shall be with him as well as they can when he suffers and dies. The Bride must share in the destiny of the Bridegroom. That is why he does not wait until he has risen from the dead to institute the Eucharist. It must happen before. There is no resurrection, either for him or for us, without a preceding death.

The Eucharist is an *intersubjective* reality. It comes about through the cooperation between Christ and the Church. Jesus does not do violence either to the bread or to the Church. It is necessary for the Church to accept that he is present in the Eucharist. Jesus as the *Real* Presence depends on the reality of Jesus' ecstatic love; it also depends on the reality of the Church's Yes. And this last reality is guaranteed for all time through the presence of Mary in the Church and her total, "immaculate" Yes.

A Decisive Choice

The disciples' (the Church's) Yes to the Eucharist is a *decisive* Yes. In the Gospel of John, we see that the Eucharist places the disciples before a definitive choice. After Jesus' great Eucharistic speech, which is presented in chapter 6, John adds: "Many of his disciples, when they heard it, said: 'This is a hard saying, who can listen to it?'" (6:60). The discourse about the Eucharist forces the disciples to take a position. Their fundamental Yes or No has to do with the Eucharist. It is the Eucharist that is the crucial point.

But the disciples *do take* a position. "Will you also go away?" Jesus asks the Twelve. Simon Peter answers in the name of all, in the name of the whole Church (he does not say: "I" but "we"). "Lord, to whom shall we go? You have the words of eternal life; and we have believed, and have come to know, that you are the Holy One of God" (6:67–69).

Since the Eucharist is the hour of sifting, it is also here, after the discourse about the Eucharist, that Jesus mentions Judas for the first time. "But there are some of you that do not believe", and John adds: "For Jesus knew from the first who those were that did not believe, and who it was that would betray him" (6:64). "Did I not choose you, the Twelve, and one of you is a devil?" (v. 70).

Diabalos comes from *diaballō*: to disperse, to divide, to separate. The one who disperses shows himself precisely at that moment when Jesus wants to unite the disciples with himself and the Father. The connection between the Eucharist and the traitor comes forth again during the Last Supper when Jesus quotes Psalm 41:10: "He who ate my bread has lifted his heel against me" (Jn 13:18), and when we hear that Satan entered into Judas when he had received the bread from Jesus (13:27). Even if the bread that Judas received is not the Eucharistic bread, it points anyway to the Eucharist. It is in connection with the Eucharist that the treachery of Judas becomes apparent.

Jesus' speech about the Eucharist forces the disciples to choose for or against Jesus. It is this speech that causes the turning point in Jesus' life, the one that exegetes usually call "the Galilean crisis". "After this many of his disciples drew back and no longer walked with him" (Jn 6:66).

John has realized more clearly than the other evangelists that the Eucharist is decisive in the Christian life. To choose Jesus is to choose the Eucharist.

The Eucharist: Christ's Sacrifice Here and Now

Just as Jesus' sacrifice on the Cross is anticipated at the Last Supper so that the sacrifice was *truly* present, so also Christ's sacrifice is truly present at every celebration of the Eucharist. Jesus' sacrifice on the Cross is a historical event. It happened once in time, but at the same time it transcends time. Christ's sacrifice has an eternal dimension. And eternity is not an endless, extended length of time, but a continuous now.

In the Eucharist, this eternal dimension becomes evident. Every time the Church celebrates the Eucharist, she goes out of time into eternity anew. She establishes herself again in the center of history and finds herself at the same time outside of history. We are allowed to be present at the sacrifice of Christ as though we were contemporary with him. Despite the fact that we come almost two thousand years later, we may nevertheless be present. John and Mary, who stood at the foot of the Cross, are not more privileged than we. The Eucharist gives us all a chance to be present at the event that is the most central one in the history of mankind.

What happened on the Cross is present in the Eucharist, in an "unbloody", but not for that reason a less realistic, manner. It becomes, rather, even more realistic. Beneath the Cross, Mary and John could not receive the life that Jesus gave for them. But we do that in the Eucharist. We are nourished by his Body and Blood.

It is certainly the *risen* Lord who is present in the Eucharist. It is his risen Body we eat, but nevertheless it is his Body as offered, sacrificed. Since Jesus offered himself on the Cross, we can never separate his person from his sacrifice. His sacrifice is the high point in his life. It is there, in his sacrifice, that he expresses perfectly in his human nature what has been within the Trinity for all eternity: the Father's Son, born of him and totally given, offered to him.

The harmony between Jesus' divine and human nature reaches its high point on the Cross. There is nothing beyond this high point. Jesus remains in this sacrificial state for all eternity. "He entered once for all into the Holy Place, taking not the blood of goats and calves but his own blood, thus securing an eternal redemption" (Heb 9:12).

This is especially clear in the Gospel of John. He sees Jesus glorified on the Cross. It is from the Cross that Jesus draws all to himself (12:32). It is he who has been "pierced" that everyone shall look upon (19:37). It is an image of eternity that John paints for us when he writes that not only blood but also water flows from the open side of Jesus, a symbol of the Spirit of glory (19:34, cf. 7:39).

Since the Eucharist is intended to give us the opportunity to participate in the sacrifice of Christ, it is also essential that this sacrifice is present. We then become immediately influenced by it. Our action becomes directly grafted onto his fundamental deed, his sacrifice to the Father for the sake of the world.

Our Christian life becomes in this way a *sacrificial* life.

The Eucharistic Ethic

Many moral theologians think that, strictly speaking, one cannot speak of a "Christian" morality. They think that morality is universal, that the same morality applies to everyone.

A Christian Ethic

Is there a specifically Christian behavior? Should a Christian act in a different way from that of a non-Christian?

The question itself perhaps causes surprise. A Christian ought to act according to the Gospel, while a non-Christian has nothing to do with the Gospel. One sometimes answers this by saying that the Gospel does not actually come with new norms, but only describes what man was intended by God to do from the beginning. The Gospel contains a true humanism. The Gospel teaches man to become completely human.

This is undeniably true, but we cannot draw from it the conclusion that there is not a specific Christian ethic.

We may not forget two things.

1. Without the Gospel, we do not know what it means to be a true human being. There is more to man than a non-Christian realizes. One can not only say *Deus semper maior* (God is always greater) but even *homo semper maior* (man is always greater). A non-Christian humanism is a limited humanism. Man is called to become one with God. "Here is the man!" (*idou ho anthropos*), says Pilate prophetically when he points to Jesus whom he allows to be scourged (Jn 19:5). One only understands what it means to be human when he looks at the Son of Man.

Here the Eucharist comes into the picture. It summarizes the whole life of Christ, all of his actions, all of his love. To look at the Son of Man is not to look at someone who lived a long time ago, to read a historical document. It is to see the Eucharist. The entire history of Christ is concentrated there.

One also notices in practice that one cannot know what it is to be a true human being without the Gospel. A non-Christian humanism looks different from the Gospel's humanism. It does not reach the same height and depth. It speaks about self-realization, while the Gospel speaks of self-forgetfulness. It speaks about satisfying one's needs, while the Gospel speaks about denying oneself.

2. Despite the fact that the message of love is also central in a non-Christian humanism, there is a radical difference between Christians and non-Christians

when it is a question of how to fulfill this command. A Christian does not only look unceasingly to Christ to learn how to love as he loves us, but he also lives in constant communion with him: he loves with his power; yes, it is he himself who loves in and through him. "It is no longer I who live, but Christ who lives in me" (Gal 2:20).

Here the Eucharist comes into the picture again. It not only shows, but also realizes the unity between man and Christ. The one who believes in the Eucharist knows that he does not stand alone. By the fact that he eats and drinks Christ, he is reminded again and again that he is one with him, that he is a branch on the vine.

A Eucharistic Ethic

When one asks a Christian: "What is man's ideal?" he cannot give an abstract answer to that question. The Christian ideal is not abstract. Abstract ideals are dangerous; they can make man fanatical and cruel. Solzhenitsyn writes in one of his books about a man who had the greatest love and respect imaginable for mankind and who just for that reason entertained a violent hatred toward every living person because they all, without exception, deformed that ideal in a terrible way.

It is often like that. The concrete person is sacrificed for the abstract ideal.

Christianity points to a concrete, living man: Jesus of Nazareth.

"Who is actually right," a correspondent asked me in a letter: "those who say that God must be in the center or those who claim that man is the center of the world?" The answer is that that is an erroneous question. We do not need to choose between God and man. The center of history and for every human life is a living person, Jesus Christ, *but this man is God*. Christianity is built on the fact that there has been a man who was completely God and completely man.

When the Church confesses that Jesus Christ is true man, it can be understood in two ways.

1. Christ is really a man like us. He does not pretend to be a man. That he is God does not mean that he is a completely different kind of human being from what we are. On the contrary, he "shared our human nature in all things but sin".[1]

2. Although it is not that which originally is meant by the words "true man", we can nevertheless interpret those words to mean that Christ is the true, perfect man. He is the man whom the human being is intended to be. He is the ideal. He shows, in a visible, concrete way, what we are called to be.

We can ask further: How and when is Jesus our example, our ideal? Is there a moment in Jesus' life when

---

[1] Fourth Eucharistic Prayer, *Daily Roman Missal*, 3rd ed. (Woodridge, Ill.: Midwest Theological Forum, 2010), 803.

in a completely special way he shows us who he is and what he wants, a moment when he expresses his inmost being, when he sums up his whole life and at the same time explains the meaning of his life?

Yes, that moment comes when he says: "This is my body given up for you. This is my blood poured out for you." It is then, precisely then, that he also says: "*Do this* in memory of me."

The Eucharist is the fundamental norm for our actions. Jesus' Eucharistic sacrifice is our ideal, our guiding principle, our rule. A rule that is much more demanding than a monastery rule, since it does not leave anything in life unaffected. When we wonder how we shall act, the answer is: "Look at the Eucharist!" There is the Christian life in its fullness.

The Christian ethic is a *Eucharistic ethic*. Jesus has instituted the Eucharist so that we will have his sacrifice in our midst as a constant source of inspiration and a clear reference point. The Eucharist is the criterion when it is a question of judging our actions! Are they or are they not in accord with the Eucharist?

Christians have always known that the Eucharist must bear fruit in daily life if one does not wish to be "a noisy gong or a clanging cymbal" (1 Cor 13:1). But in the last decades, the Church has become evermore aware that the Eucharist is intended to penetrate *everything* we do.

The All-Embracing Meaning of the Eucharist

The Eucharist is a summary of Christ's *entire* life. That is why it can also be a concrete, absolute, and exhaustive rule *for our entire lives*. If the Eucharist had represented only a limited period in Christ's life, it would not have the all-embracing meaning that we attach to it. In reality, the Eucharist is a synthesis of Jesus' life in its entirety.

This becomes easier to understand if we realize that the New Testament, in particular Saint John, considers the whole life of Christ as a meal that he eats together with the people.

Let us go through some of the meals that John describes in his Gospel.

"On the third day there was a *marriage at Cana* in Galilee" (Jn 2:1; emphasis added). "On the third day" alludes, of course, to the Resurrection that happens on the third day. It is clear from the beginning that this wedding has something to do with the Resurrection. If one reads the text carefully (Jn 1:19–51), one discovers that this "third day" is at the same time the seventh and last day in the first week that introduces Jesus' public life and that in some way is an anticipated synthesis of Jesus' whole life. What happens on the last day of the week finishes and completes everything that has happened during the course of the week. It sets the seal on his work.

The first week receives its completion at a *meal*. The disciples and "Jesus' Mother" understand that this meal is a sign: "This, the first of his signs, Jesus did . . ." (2:11). It is a sign of the messianic meal where Jesus is the true Bridegroom. In a veiled way, Jesus already celebrates a wedding with his Church.

This first sign is a kind of archetype that sums up Jesus' life. The story of his life is the story of his wedding with the Church. That is why a wedding feast can symbolize his life.

In Cana, Jesus' hour has not yet come (2:4). Mary and the disciples hear that "the hour" lies in the future, that what happens here is still not the definitive hour, but only anticipates it. "The good wine" (2:10) portends a still better wine that Jesus will offer in the Eucharist, and that is his Blood. From the very beginning, the Eucharist is there in the Gospel of John.

While the wedding at Cana took place on the last day of the first week, the *meal at Bethany* happens "six days before the Passover" (Jn 12:1), that is, the first day of the last week. Both weeks, the first and the last, are a summary of Jesus' life.

By letting Jesus' public life begin and end with a meal, John wants to demonstrate that Jesus' whole life is a meal. The meal is Alpha and Omega in his life.

The meal in Bethany portends Christ's death. What happens on the first day of the last week already contains in a hidden way the whole week's course of events. Mary, the sister of Lazarus and Martha, anoints

Jesus' feet with expensive nard balsam. Jesus responds to Judas' criticism with: "Let her alone, let her keep it for *the day of my burial*" (Jn 12:7; emphasis added).

The meal at Bethany has its corresponding counterpart at the Last Supper. In Bethany, Mary anoints Jesus' feet. In Jerusalem, it is Jesus who washes the disciples' feet. There is a mutuality of love and service between the Bridegroom and the Bride, between Jesus and the Church.

Jesus gives his long farewell discourse during *a last meal*. "During supper" (13:2), writes Saint John. All five chapters of John's Gospel have in their own way a clear character of a meal.

A detailed analysis of the farewell discourse shows, according to exegetes, that it recapitulates the whole Gospel, not for great crowds of people now, but only for the disciples in the intimate atmosphere of a last farewell meal. The Last Supper summarizes Jesus' whole life, which once again shows that we may consider Jesus' life as a meal.

This last meal represents a wedding feast like the first in Cana. The disciple "whom Jesus loved", the type for every disciple and for the whole Church, lies on the "breast of Jesus" (13:23). The Greek word *kolpos* means both breast and bosom.

Even *after his Resurrection*, Jesus wants to eat with his disciples. It is he himself who arranges the meal: "When they got out on land, they saw a charcoal fire there, with fish lying on it, and bread" (Jn 21:9).

"Come and have breakfast", he says (v. 12). The choice of words is such that one cannot miss the Eucharistic atmosphere. "Jesus came and took the bread and gave it to them, and so with the fish" (v. 13). The evangelist uses exactly the same words in the description of the miracle of the loaves (6:1–15), which itself is a clear symbol of the Eucharist.

John describes Jesus' life as a meal. This is extremely meaningful. It makes it possible for us to enter not only into a part of Jesus' life, namely, his suffering, death, and Resurrection, but into *all* of his life through the Eucharist. The Eucharist is a synthesis of *Jesus'* whole life and can also regulate and guide *our* whole lives.

The Eucharist is the source of a specific Christian behavior on all levels. It regulates all of our relations: (1) our relation to God: to be totally offered to him and live in constant thanksgiving; (2) our relation to each other: to be each other's servants; (3) our relation to nature and the world: to consider and use them so that they reveal something of God's glory.

Nothing lies outside of the influential sphere of the Eucharist. The answer to the question: "How shall I live?" ought always to be: "live Eucharistically!"

In the spring of 1989, I gave a retreat to the Sisters in Turku, Finland. The retreat was about the Eucharist. After one of the conferences, Birgit Klockars, the learned historian and scholar of Saint Bridget of Sweden, came up to me and gave me the following poem. It struck me that the poem expressed so exactly what I had tried to convey during the retreat. Later I came to know that the poem was written in the fall of 1946, when she had just come home from China the first time and was in the process of ending her involvement with the Salvation Army. She had not yet seriously discovered the Church and the Eucharist!

~

Broken Bread

You blessed the bread and broke it
to the satisfaction of people in need,
and the multitudes ate it and rejoiced.
Perhaps they would have fainted from hunger
if the bread had not been broken.

Bless me also and break me,
if in that way you can use me
for the gladness and joy of others.
You gave yourself to be broken
for our salvation, Man of sorrows.

(Du välsignade brödet och bröt det
till mättnad för människor i nöd,
och skarorna åt det och gladdes.
Av hunger de kanske försmäktat,
om det varit ett obrutet bröd.

Välsigna mig också och bryt mig,
Om så du mig använda kan
till hugnad och glädje för andra.
Du gav ju dig själv till att brytas
för vår frälsning, Smärtornas man.)